WILD BIRDS

WILD BIRDS

*Field Notes
of a Wildlife Psychologist*

Carl Pickhardt Ph.D.

To order additional copies of this book, contact:
Xlibris Corporation
1-888-795-4274
www.Xlibris.com
Orders@Xlibris.com
15246

CONTENTS

To Dr. Esteban,
the blind bird watcher,
who set me this exercise in imagination:

"Draw one hundred birds you cannot see,
make up a name for every one,
then state the lesson each creation has to teach."

PREFACE

We can create devices that will fly.
We can build vehicles in which to fly.
But we cannot make our bodies fly.

At most,
We dive free-falling down
Toward the swiftly rising ground,
Or float or glide,
Soar or ride
On artificial wings and things
Attached to us but not of us,
And so as we succeed,
We fail.

Which is perhaps why,
Earthbound as we are,
We envy and admire birds
For their freedom in the air,
For the glory of their flight,
For the magic of their contrivance,
And for the beauty and variety of their design,
Which is the subject of this book:
A tribute in line and words
To the elegance of birds.

From one fellow creature to another.

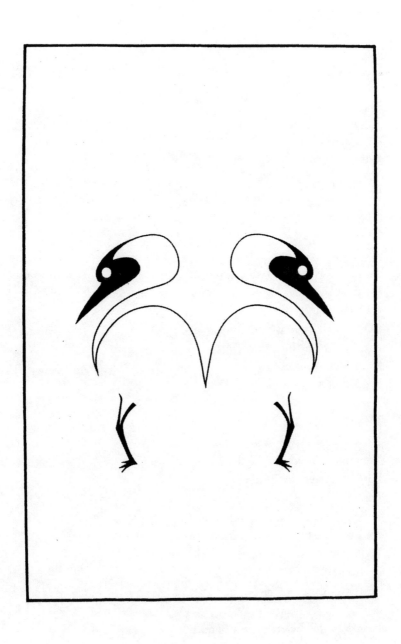

THE COURTSHIP

Who choreographs the dance of courtship,
Different for each kind of bird,
And how are interested parties
Taught the multiplicity of steps?

Tipping and tilting,
Stamping and kicking,
Tail raising and tail flipping,
Flying up and fluttering down,
Weaving about each other in the air,
Wings spreading and wings quivering,
Chasing around in circles on the ground,
Calling to attract and calling to respond,
Modulating tone and varying song,
Making music for their dance,
Breeding when ritual is done.

Without instruction,
How do they come to know
What neither has been shown or rehearsed?

Knowledge too important to entrust
To the hit or miss of education
Is encoded in each bird.

Instinct, we call it:
How to feed and how to fly,
How to court and how to mate,
How to bathe and how to preen,
How to flock and how to migrate,
How to mark territory and defend,
How to build a nest and raise a brood.

Birds are born so well prepared to survive,
While humans start innately ill-equipped.
Yet though beginning knowing less,
We end by understanding more.

Learning compensates at last
For our ignorance at first.

INCUBATION

"What are you doing?"
"Sitting around."
"Anything happening?"
"Not that I can tell."
"So how long are you going to sit and wait?"
"For however long it takes."

Exactly.

The time required to incubate
Is not up to the incubator,
But to the eggs,
A lesson writers learn
When they make efforts to create
Yet nothing productive will come out.

"I've hit a wall."
"I've run out of ideas."
"I can't figure what comes next."

But getting stuck isn't what it seems.
Just as you're getting nowhere
With a mental block that won't give way,
You're getting somewhere if you won't give up.

Impasses are part of the creative process,
Faith in that process what is required.

Stay committed and a door will open,
Stay committed and insight will emerge,
Not exactly on your schedule,
But in its own sweet time.

THE CHICK

Such a rude awakening,
From dark confinement to bright confusion.

Blind to the sudden light,
What does the *Chick* want to know?

"Where am I?"
You are in the here and now.
"What am I supposed to do?"
To survive the best you can.
And another struggle for life begins
As the shell is broken open and cast aside.

Or is it?

Not if every shell is nested in a larger shell
And birth (like death) is a transition into another.
Then every shell is only temporary,
Only a way station for further change.

As the world keeps changing
It keeps changing us as we keep up,
Just as our keeping up changes the world.

Change doesn't cease because change cannot stop.
Change didn't start because change always was.
Change is the only thing that doesn't change.

There was no beginning and there will be no end.
There is only change—the shell of shells around us all.

THE FLEDGLING

One can almost imagine the parents
Wanting to scream back:
"WILL YOU GROW UP!"
To the *Fledgling* who is out of their nest,
But not out of their lives,
Not ready to dispense with their services,
Following them about with furiously flapping wings
Demanding to be fed until,
To gain momentary relief from this relentless pursuit,
One parent regurgitates a little something
Into their son's or daughter's begging mouth
To shut the squawking up.

Weaning fills the time
Between holding on and letting go,
And the timing is rarely right.

Parents can be ready for self-sufficiency in a child
Who still feels wed to dependency on them.
Or a child can be ready to break free of parents
Who are reluctant to release the controls of care.

Fortunately,
Because they parent sequentially,
Adult birds have to finish with one brood
Before hatching the next.

Not like people,
Who also parent sequentially,
Except "in with the new"
Does not mean "out with the old."

Only the addition of more.

For human beings just as birds, however,
Weaning brutally comes down to this:
"It's time to
Sustain yourself,
Protect yourself,
And find your own home."

THE YOUNG ADULT

To become adult is not the same
As being all grown up
Because reaching adulthood
Is not the end of growth.

Becoming adult
Just matches full physical capacity
With the responsibility for self-sufficiency,
The bird relinquishing dependence on parents
Who relinquish taking care of it.

Of course there's more to learn of life
Than has been learned so far,
But parents
(Particularly of the human kind)
May get impatient with the *Young Adult*,
Name-calling youthful ignorance "stupidity."

But not knowing isn't stupid, it is wise,
Because ignorance is knowledge in disguise.

The more one knows,
The more one knows
How much one doesn't know;
The more one knows
Not knowing shows
What there remains to know;
The more one knows

Not knowing grows
The more one comes to know;
The more one knows
Without not knowing
No one wants to know;
The more one knows
It's stupid not to know
One doesn't know.

CLASSIFICATION

It's hard for the novice bird watcher
To distinguish kinds of birds from one another.

For example,
To the untutored eye,
The *Rock-tailed Ringwort*
And the *Ring-tailed Ratwink*
Look exactly alike unless one knows
Under the Ringwort's left wing is a splash of yellow,
While under the Ratwink's right wing is a blush of pink,
An obvious distinction to experts,
Mysterious to those who aren't.

Why can't we just leave similarity alone
And let gross distinctions be enough?

But no,
We can't be satisfied a bird's identified
Unless we describe and subdivide,
Describe and subdivide,
Breaking the smallest collective down
Until apparent duplicates appear unlike.

Is this what classification is about?
We can't know anything for sure,
Until we can tell everything apart.

THE MULL

One wonders if the *Mull* ever sleeps
Given the constant watch it keeps
Over its personal space,
Patrolling other birds away.

Of course,
By walling others out,
The Mull walls itself in,
Prisoner of what it must defend.

The problem with being a 'Have'
Is holding onto what one has
That others lack and want
But cannot get.

At least not yet.

Division is particularly divisive
When profound inequity results,
Often creating conflict over who owns what.

Then in the war
Between who has
And who has not,
The outcome may surprise
As the gifts of adversity prevail
Over the privileges of advantage,
Those with less fighting harder
Than those with more.

After all,
Who develops a stronger will?
Those accustomed to the comforts of power
Or those inured to challenges of hardship?
Those with everything at stake
Or those with nothing left to lose?

THE SCURRIED WADRELL

How does the *Scurried Wadrell*
Keep its balance when awake,
Much less asleep,
Head pillowed on its back,
One leg tucked underneath,
One leg to stand upon
Without a wobble or a sway,
Not tipping over and falling down?

Maintaining stability
Requires practice, judgment, and restraint,
Not drawn off center by being drawn to an extreme,
Balance—the art of living in between
All or nothing
(Being content with *some*)
Now or never
(Being content with *later*)
Yes or no
(Being content with *perhaps*)

Best or worst
(Being content with *average*)
Wonderful or awful
(Being content with *adequate*)
Excess or abstinence
(Being content with *moderation*)
My way or your way
(Being content with *compromise*)
Black or white
(Being content with *gray*.)

To keep balance,
Follow the middle way.

THE KISKATOON

Whether perching, hopping, or in flight,
The *Kiskatoon* communicates delight.
Is happiness its natural state?
Perhaps.
But not for us.
Only naturally desired.

But seeking a single path to contentment,
We discover there are many instead of one.

Working hard or being lazy,
Acting responsibly or acting crazy,
Being served or being of service,
Pleasing oneself or pleasing others,
Being in danger or being secure,
Causing conflict or keeping peace,
Being obedient or being rebellious,
Getting love or giving love,
Being ideal or being real,
Living lavishly or living simply,
Being ambitious or being content,
Being entertained or entertaining oneself,

Being with others or being alone,
Being still or being busy,
Being quiet or being loud,
Doing one's duty or doing one's pleasure,
Having faith or having money,
Being serious or being funny,
Holding a grudge or granting forgiveness,
Being noticed or being ignored,
Being famous or being unknown,
Having order or having clutter,
Getting to win or getting to play,
Getting along or getting one's way.

Happiness is different for different people,
What one finds pleasing displeasing to another.

THE TAPALAC

Taking life as it comes,
The *Tapalac* simply awaits
Whatever the future brings,
But that's not good enough for us.

We want to be prepared,
So we devise a host of strategies
To influence
And to anticipate
What happens next
Into doing what we want,
Into being what we thought,
By satisfying our assumptions,
By conforming to our conditions,
By meeting our expectations,
By following our directions,
By obeying our laws,
By reaching our goals,
By fitting into our plans,
By fulfilling our predictions,
By validating our hypotheses,

By maintaining our routines,
By observing our traditions,
By performing our rituals,
By repeating our habits,
By pursuing our dreams,
By indulging our worries,
By reducing our risks,
By granting our wishes,
By answering our prayers,
By justifying our faith,
By winning a lucky guess,
By confirming a superstition,
By obeying the law of averages,
By striving to create some certainty
In a world ruled by infinite unknowns.

THE TAUP

The *Taup*
Rides out the roughest sea.
Battered by breakers,
It preserves its buoyancy.

After a curling wave comes crashing down,
The Taup swims lightly through the seething foam.

Somehow the ocean's fury leaves the little bird unscathed.

This concession to a fragile creature is instructive:
No force of nature is entirely destructive.

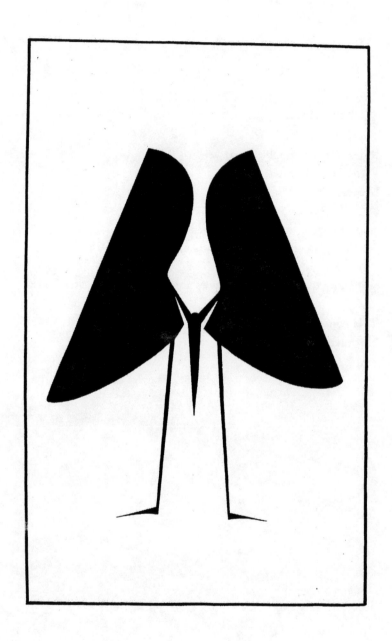

THE BLACK WING

"A bird on stilts"
Is how the *Black Wing's* been described:
Stiff-legged and spear-billed,
Wings barely large enough
To lift it off the ground,
Ponderously swimming through the air,
Landing gear lazily stretching out behind.

But the *Black Wing*
Doesn't mind what humans say
Because humans act peculiar in their way—
Clothing themselves in artificial dress,
Destroying habitat to make their ugly nests,
Creating endless stuff that only leaves a mess,
Wasting time by trying to make sense,
Making foes,
Making war,
Making peace,
Making friends,
Making enemies,
So that it's time to fight again,
Never giving nature's health a second thought,
Although it's nature's health on which they all depend.

How other creatures look to us
Is nowhere near as strange
As we must look to them.

THE JOJO

With its saucer eyes and steady stare,
The *Jojo* has no time for future or for past
Because a single moment is immeasurably vast,
Encompassing a world of simultaneous events
Compelling full attention
From the creature's present sense.

Hard to be human
And be so currently aware
Except in infancy when every instant is truly amazing
And in adolescence when *the rule of now* returns—
Impulse ignoring childish restraints,
Living like there's no tomorrow,
Resenting limits and demands,
Frustrated by discussion and delay,
Wanting what is wanted
When it's wanted
Which is right away
Because all that matters is today.

Growing up is giving up:
As maturity is gained,
Immediacy is lost.

THE WICKETT

In ancient times
The *Wickett* was a fortune-telling bird
Whose behavior when interpreted by the oracular
Could signify and prophesy events.

A good sign
When a Wickett called
Within twelve hours of a child's birth:
Prosperity ahead.

A bad sign
When a flock of Wicketts
Huddled on a single tree:
An omen of calamity instead.

Of course,
In our more enlightened age
We aren't gulled by superstition anymore.
Imagine: soothsaying power in a bird!

We are too practical.
We are too realistic.
We are too wise.

Now we believe what sellers advertise.

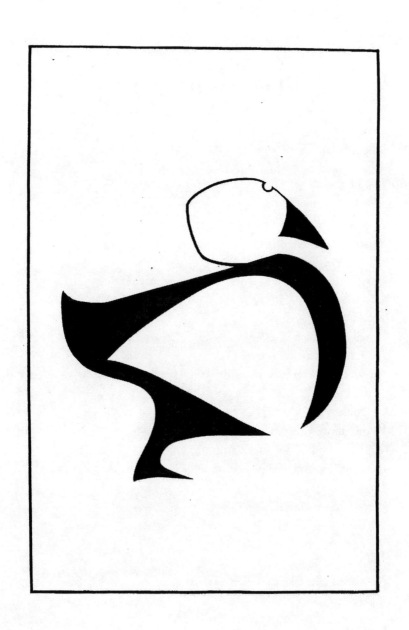

THE McPADDEN

Why does the *McPadden* go back
To the scene of attack?
Surely escaping with its life
Should discourage risking a return.

Can't it remember?
Didn't it learn?

Yes and yes.
But mental states
Are neither independent nor discrete.

Another side of fear is fascination.
(What's frightening also has allure.)

Another side of anger is valuing.
(We don't get mad unless we care.)

Another side of giving up is letting go.
(When we stop trying, we stop holding on.)

Another side of grief is gratitude.
(Mourning celebrates the gift of what was lost.)

Another side of worry is imagination.
(Asking "What if?" is an act of make-believe.)

Another side of frustration is persistence.
(We still keep wanting what we've yet to get.)

Another side of complaining is motivation.
(Unless we're discontent, we've no desire for change.)

Another side of prohibition is temptation.
(The forbidden is laden with desire.)

Another side of hate is attachment.
(Abhorrence is a passionate connection.)

By extension,
Every mental state
Is related to another.

THE SKIMMER

With a few quick flaps and a swooping glide,
A few quick flaps and a swooping glide,
The *Skimmer* surfs
The undulating land
In roller-coaster flight,
Rising high and dipping low,
Enjoying the swift and easy ride,
Feeding occasionally upon the fly,
Resting occasionally on a passing tree,
The little bird a model of pure tranquility.

How does it live so carefree?

It doesn't own much, it doesn't owe much.
It doesn't eat much, it doesn't crave much.
It doesn't plan much, it doesn't hope much.
It doesn't envy much, it doesn't worry much.
It doesn't aspire much, it doesn't strive much.
It doesn't blame much, it doesn't resent much.
It doesn't regret much, it doesn't mourn much.
It doesn't defend much, it doesn't attack much.
It doesn't demand much, it doesn't control much.
It doesn't complain much, it doesn't criticize much.

It doesn't take life too personally.
It doesn't take life too seriously.
It doesn't take life for granted.
It just goes with the flow
And goes its own way.

THE CAPED MACAWL

Prized by collectors of exotic pets,
The *Caped Macawl* outlives all other birds,
Even its human keepers
Who admire
Its acrobatic grip,
Its adaptable beak,
Its brilliant plumage,
Its mimicry of sound,
And its fabled longevity.

Hard not to venerate long life
Since it gives hope
To the dream of immortality,
Except immortality is also real.

Material decay
Is just alteration,
Not passing away.

It's not that anything is permanent,
It's just that nothing entirely ceases to exist.

Everything gone in one form
Stays around in another.

Everything *was* actually *is*
And everything *is* actually *was*.

Everything young is actually old.
Everything old is soon to be young.

Nothing's forever,
But everything lasts.

THE RUDDY DABBLER

Hissing and clucking,
Glaring and flapping,
Charging and challenging,
The *Ruddy Dabbler*
Does it's duty:
Warning off danger,
Safeguarding its family,
Risking injury to protect its young.

What dedication does it take to parent?

Putting children first and setting oneself aside.
Providing what they can't for themselves.
Doing without so they may have enough.
Working on when energy is spent.
Hanging in there and not giving up.
Thinking ahead
When they can only think of now.
Stating opinions they do not want to hear.
Imposing limits and demands they may resent.
Being blamed for disallowing their desires.
Letting go as they go on their own.
At last being left at home alone.

Making a child does not make a parent.
Years of effort and sacrifice are what it takes.

THE SPEE

How does the *Spee*
Know how to be a bird?

Because it is one.

Any creature's nature
Limits and prescribes the way it acts.

All right.

Then on what terms
Are human creatures meant to live?

Here's the deal:
Life is a given with no guarantees;
We have to learn to do it as we grow;
Most of what happens we won't control;
Much we do right others will deem wrong;
We'll rarely satisfy our need to know enough;
We'll make mistakes we wish we could correct;
We'll have to live with everything we've done;
We'll get outcomes we often don't expect;
We'll improvise more than we'll plan;
And we'll end up as ignorant as we began,
Like infants wondering just what comes next.

THE PRAIRIE LONGBILL

What's a bird the size of a swan
Doing wading in a place like this?
In seasonal shallows meant for migratory ducks,
The *Prairie Longbill* stands out like an interloper
That doesn't fit in,
That doesn't belong,
That doesn't conform,
That should be set apart,
That should be kept away,
That should be driven off except it's not.

If the proverbial wisdom is correct
And "birds of a feather flock together,"
Then birds who are "different"
Should stick to their own kind.

Is this gathering place
Around a common need
Nature's way of mixing creatures up
So they can learn to share and get along?

We have more trouble with our own diversity.

How differences are viewed becomes one key.
"I'm different from you" or "You're different from me."
Either can imply inferior status or superiority.
Comparisons are odious indeed.

"We are different from each other,"
Respects individuality.

When differences prevent association,
Ignorance can teach what isn't so.
When differences are cause for enmity,
We/They distinctions can justify a war.
When differences are bridges to understanding,
We can cross over and appreciate each other more.

Differences are really similarities.
Opposition over contending beliefs
Means we both value believing.

Beneath our great diversity,
A greater sameness connects us all.

THE NORTHERN CLINGER

Detecting hidden life beneath the bark,
The *Northern Clinger* bores the outer skin
Only to discover food has tunneled further in.

Undeterred,
The persistent bird
Begins to drill the body of the tree
Mining for an insect it cannot see
But may eventually find,
Using its head
As well as its mind,
In a determined effort,
With no outcome guaranteed.

That getting fed is not assured
Is not a problem but how existence is.
The bird does its level best
And whatever happens
Or doesn't happen
Does the rest.

Despite sense of destiny or entitlement,
The same reality holds true for us.

In this chancy world,
There's no adversity to overcome,
Only challenges to meet and master if we can,
And if we can't then learn from our defeat
To live on terms we may not like,
We can't control or change,
But can choose to accept,
From acceptance,
Creating our content.

THE COASTAL TERN

High soaring, long-winged, keen seeing,
Swift dropping, down swooping, sea skimming,
Plunge diving, bill stabbing, fish plucking,
Slow rising, strong toting, rock landing,
Feast eating, fast sleeping, quick waking,
Food needing, sky climbing, high soaring:
Each day the *Coastal Tern* hunts to live,
As must we all.

We may not hunt for game,
But we are hunters all the same:
We hunt for answers,
We hunt for solutions,
We hunt for truth,
We hunt for meaning,
We hunt for approval,
We hunt for recognition,
We hunt for work,
We hunt for what is lost,
We hunt for the least cost,
We hunt for escape,
We hunt for excitement,
We hunt for adventure,
We hunt for treasure,
We hunt for pleasure
We hunt for glory,
We hunt for love,
We hunt for peace of mind.

We may not hunt to kill,
But we always hunt to find.

THE SAND HATCHER

What kind of parent is a *Sand Hatcher*?
Laying eggs on a scrape of ground,
Leaving chicks unattended to go off and feed,
Returning to its casual nest perhaps hoping for the best,
To find its young spared or plundered,
Child safety left to happenstance.

Of course,
When we leave our offspring alone
Or when they leave us behind,
We too leave them to chance
Or they take chances of their own,
Luck the great protector and victimizer
Of children's vulnerability,
Responsible for miraculous survivals,
Harrowing near misses,
And tragic outcomes
That disable and destroy young lives.

What parents control is not the child but themselves:
The love they give,
The skills they teach,
The demands they make,
The values they promote,
The examples they model,
The restraints they impose,
The information they share,
The treatment they provide,
All have formative but finite effect.

Consider all that they are helpless to direct:
The child's given nature,
The child's rate of growth,
The persuasive power of peers,
The personal choices the child makes,
The cultural content of the child's world,
The models and messages the media sends,
The chance events that rule the child's daily life.

Parents have limited effect
Over how their child "turns out."
Easy to take credit for what they do not deserve,
Easy to shoulder guilt for what was not their fault.
To assume total responsibility is to assume too much.

THE WORRET

Perched on the end of anywhere
Accepting anything that happens,
The *Worret* takes experience as it unfolds,
As if to say:
"Whatever came last,
Whatever comes next,
Whatever disrupts,
Whatever connects,
Whatever goes well,
Whatever goes bad,
Whatever one gets,
Whatever one had,
Whatever change brings,
Whatever change takes,
Whatever befalls,
Whatever mistakes,
Life is as it is
And I am as I am."

But being human,
We want more than this,
So we ask fundamental questions
In hopes sound answers will provide
Some explanations to make sense of our experience:
"Why is life?
How does it work?
How should we act?
Why does it matter?"

Who knows?

Life has no cause,
Life has no order,
Life has no purpose,
Life has no meaning,
Life has no value,
Life has no scruples,
Save for whatever
Cause and order,
Purpose and meaning,
Value and scruples,
We religiously,
We philosophically,
We scientifically suppose.

THE GREATER SAWBILL

When hunting fails to produce
And intended prey escapes again,
The Greater Sawbill is calmly undeterred.

A persistent bird,
It doesn't curse its fate,
It doesn't get discouraged,
It doesn't feel disappointed,
It doesn't envy those with better luck,
It doesn't complain about being treated unfairly,
It doesn't act like Life owes it a living,
It doesn't feel deprived of happiness,
It doesn't feel sorry for itself,
It doesn't indulge self-pity,
It doesn't complain "Poor me!"
It doesn't question the point of trying,
It doesn't consider giving up and going out on strike.

Why not?

Because it knows that trying
Is one difference between living and dying,
That good fortune is a hit and miss proposition,
That both success and failure can result from effort,
That it controls effort but not outcome,
That keeping on keeps hope alive,
That life is a struggle
And is meant to be.
That's the reason for adversity.

So, why not give up the fight?

Because if you don't play you can't win,
But if you do play,
You just might.

THE CRESCENT SCROON

Rarely observed because it's really rare,
The *Crescent Scroon* excites observers when seldom seen,
Particular attention paid to this occurrence of infrequency.

But is this special valuing deserved?

Are the occasional worth more than the common?
Are the unusual worth more than the ordinary?
Are the exceptions worth more than the rule?
Are the few worth more than the many?

Discount the familiar
And cause for wonder is diminished.

It's when every creature,
Every object,
Every moment,
Every experience,
Rare or routine,
Scarce or plentiful,
Becomes a source of enlightenment
That life becomes as rich as it deserves to be.

Because everything
Is unique to some degree,
Everything is a case of rarity.

THE AMACORD

Unlike the *Amacord*
Who accepts reality,
We cling to wishful thinking
Hoping to make our wishes true.

There is forever.
No: only as long as something lasts.
There is returning to a simpler time.
No: only coping with growing complexity.
There are some acts that don't matter.
No: everything counts because everything contributes.
There is reform that can start tomorrow.
No: change can only begin today.
There is a final answer.
No: only the latest understanding.
There's an infinite supply.
No: only limited amounts.
There is throwing things away.
No: only moving things around.
There is an easy solution to hard problems.
No: only hard compromises to be made.
There is mind reading between intimates.
No: only knowing from actually being told.
There are isolated acts.
No: only interdependent events.
There is control over others.
No: only others giving us consent.
There is free love.

No: only limiting freedom for the sake of commitment.
There is leaving our past behind.
No: only learning to live with our history.
There is happily ever after.
No: only the ups and downs of what comes next.
There is peace for all time.
No: only peace some of the time.

Part of being human is believing in illusions.

THE SCARP

"Follow the leader" is not simply a child's game,
But adult behavior too serious for play:
How the many cede control over their lives to one,
Going along with what he or she wants done,
Assuming that what works for the best of them
Will work for the rest of them,
Like a flight of *Scarp*
Strung out behind a single bird
Who determines everyone's direction for good or ill,
Followed by those who can't find the way but believe another will.

But how do leaders persuade?
Usually with strategies that work on themselves.

If logic and reason, they tend to explain.
If obedience and deference, they tend to command.
If dishonesty and deception, they tend to manipulate.
If will and force, they tend to coerce.
If fear and dread, they tend to intimidate.
If criticism and shame, they tend to humiliate.
If guilt and obligation, they tend to extort.
If love and acceptance, they tend to respect.
If collaboration and trust, they tend to involve.
If approval and appreciation they tend to reward.

Leaders don't actually lead people.
They lead themselves and others choose to follow.

Therefore, to be a beneficial leader for yourself:
Lead your life like someone you'd admire,
Whose example you would want to model,
Whose good regard you'd want to earn,
Whose commitments you could trust,
Who words would tell the truth,
From whom you could learn
To become an even "better person"
In the best sense of that complicated term.

THE ARCTIC SCREE

Who'd want to live in a place like this?

It takes a stout resolve
And a strong constitution
To roost upon the rocky arctic coast,
To endure the unrelenting arctic freeze,
To withstand the chilling arctic blast,
To fish in the frigid arctic sea,
And yet the *Arctic Scree*
Sees nothing harsh about this habitat,
And other birds can live elsewhere they like.

Such are the differences that set creatures apart.

What is inhospitable for one is home for another.
What is inedible for one is delicious for another.
What is difficult for one is easy for another.
What is repelling for one is attractive for another.
What is risky for one is routine for another.
What is confusing for one is clear for another.
What is worthless for one is of value for another.
What is intolerable for one is welcome for another.
What is foolish for one is serious for another.
What is wrong for one is right for another.
What is blasphemous for one is holy for another.

No wonder differences cause all the conflicts they do,
Constantly creating opposing points of view.

THE SEEDEATER

It's tempting to share a crust
With the *Seedeater* begging at my feet,
Offering proximity for something to eat,
The bargain made by all degrees of pets
As we exploit their hungry need,
We hunger for benefits
Domestication offers in return.

By providing feed,
We get service,
We get affection,
We get entertainment,
We get companionship,
We get sustenance back.

But taming them,
We also tame ourselves
Because as they lose wildness,
We lose exposure to what was wild.

By creating this domestic captivity,
We are obliged to those who now depend on us.

Thus the keeper becomes prisoner of the kept.

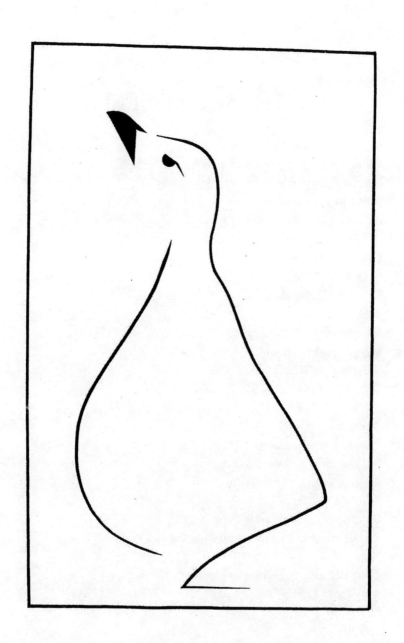

THE STARRY GAWKER

Why is the *Starry Gawker* always staring at the sky?
Searching for inspiration of some kind?
Is there a rare celestial event to see?
Or is it keeping a weather eye out for inclemency?

Most other birds spend more time looking down than up,
Grounded in day to day concerns
For keeping fed,
For keeping safe,
For keeping clean,
For keeping mating,
For keeping territory,
For keeping going when the going's tough,
Just keeping busy because survival's hard enough.

Why should any creature bother
With theory, possibility, or history,
With purpose, principles, or morality?
They just make living more demanding and complex.

Who cares about
The how or why or when or should of what occurs?
We do: because we can't resist attaching meaning to reality.

When we named the first object,
When we conceived the first idea,
When we asked the first question,
When we gave the first answer,
When we posed the hypothesis,
When we confirmed the first prediction,
When we exalted the first ideal,
When we condemned the first wrong,
When we disputed the first belief,
When we developed the first tradition,
When we worshipped the first deity,
When we invented the first technology,
When we created the first art,
What we gained was to our everlasting cost:
For the wonderful gifts of rationality,
Relative simplicity was lost.

THE BLUE BACK

When the earth is torn apart by drought,
Cracking deeper as the moisture is sucked out,
Riverbeds turn into old dirt roads
And dry lakes into craters filled with dust.

When water disappears then water worlds are lost,
Then life within those worlds is lost as well,
Then the *Blue Back* loses a source of food
And migrates to a wetter place to live.

Why do we remain?
Because we can find water when it doesn't rain,
Because we're independent of the river and the lake,
Except human independence simply isn't so.

We create a house of cards in which to live,
Then act surprised when it is tumbled down
Because the winter storms,
Because the blizzard blankets,
Because the snow drifts,
Because the avalanches,
Because the cold freezes,
Because the gale blows,
Because the wind shears,
Because the cyclones,
Because the downpours,
Because the flash floods,
Because the seas fill,

Because the tides rise,
Because the breakers crash,
Because the shore sinks,
Because the mud slides,
Because the sun dries,
Because the heat waves,
Because the lightening strikes,
Because the forest fires,
Because the sky pales,
Because the hail stones,
Because the twister hits,
And the earth quakes,
And the tidal waves,
And the glacier flows,
And the volcano blows,
Because we're all subject to Nature's rule.

THE PICONI

Some birds are tense,
Ever alert for a surprise,
In a hurry to be moving on,
Distracted by something new,
Soon dissatisfied by how things are,
But the *Piconi* stays immune to stress
By simply living within its means to do,
Content if life provides it with sufficiency,
Unlike people who much prefer excess.

We do so many tasks at once,
We do none of them very well.
We start so many projects,
We can't finish them all.
We create so many choices,
We can't make up our minds.
We are tempted by so much,
We stick at nothing very long.
We get so used to changing,
Without variety we're bored.
We hear so many experts,
We become confused.

We lose sight of lasting value
In our hunger for the news.
We commit to do so much,
We feel pressured to catch up.
We build systems so complex,
They are hard to understand.
We regulate so much,
We feel helpless to control.
We ordain so many rules,
We curse restrictions they impose.
We glut on information,
Retaining less as slippage grows.

We fill our lives with more than they can hold,
And then feel victim of abundance and overload.

THE SENTINEL

When the *Sentinel* looks ahead,
Exactly what's it looking forward to?

Better times?
The unexpected?
Some hope or dread?

What about looking back,
Guarding against a sneak attack?

That's the problem with focus,
We can't look opposing ways at once:
In and out,
Up and down,
Back and forth,
Here and there,
Or everywhere at a single glance.

Each moment we must choose what to attend.

For example:
In our current state,
Do we reminisce or anticipate,
Do we dwell on yesterday or ponder tomorrow?

How much of our present do we invest
In considering our future
Or in contemplating our past?

For the young,
With less past accrued,
The future holds a wealth of possibilities.

For the old,
With less future remaining,
The past becomes a trove of memories.

As we age,
Our focus tends to shift
From what has latest interest
To what has lasting value for us now.

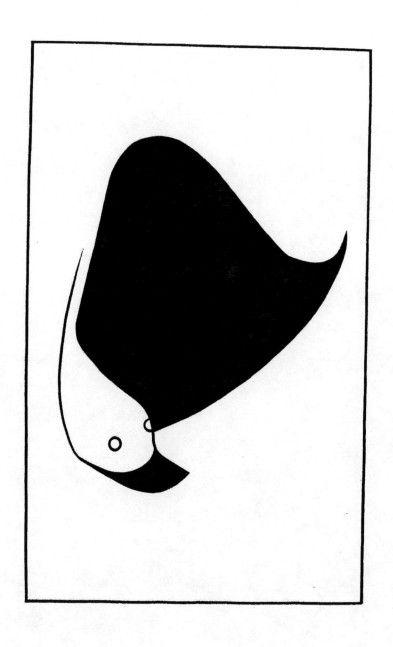

THE QUESTALL

Why does the *Questall* need to know
More than it needs to know
To satisfy its basic needs
Unless like us
It has a drive to find things out,
A drive we can't explain but can't deny?

Either our curiosity is very high
Or our tolerance for ignorance is very low,
Or the unknown makes us feel afraid,
Or we crave information for its own sake,
Or our minds demand constant data to be fed,
Or without fresh ideas we cannot seem to think,
Or knowledge helps us feel more in control,
Or we must determine facts to feel secure,
Or we can't resist discovery's allure,
Or we simply love the chance to learn,
Or we need to stay informed to still belong,
Or we need to tell and to be told to keep in touch:
Who knows why we need to know so much?

Even the simplest greeting
Is an effort to find out:
"How are you?"
"What's going on?"
"Where have you been?"

Our need to know:
Where will it end?

And why did it begin?

THE WILDFOWL

Amazing how the *Wildfowl*
Finds its way from Mexico to Canada and back,
Seasonally feeding at one locale,
Seasonally breeding at the other,
Seasonally leaving when the time feels right,
Flying thousands of miles over unknown terrain
Because the flyway is slightly different every time,
Although both destinations remain the same,
Each destination a departure point
From which migration soon begins again.

How does the Wildfowl know
When to leave and where to go?
And why this yearning for returning
Instead of journeying to someplace new?

Because someplace new is really someplace old,
Because no matter what the migratory move,
Habits command us to repeat ourselves,
Because no matter where we go
We keep bringing ourselves along,
Because despite the geographic shift
How we began remains most of how we become,
Because history shapes our future with our sense of past,
Because external change is no match for internal consistency.

So perhaps in each of us
A clock and compass are crudely set
Assigning a schedule and direction
To our migratory path through life
That we only understand as it unfolds
Season to season and year to year,
Revealed most clearly at the very end.

"Yes, that's what my life has been about."

"Yes, now I begin to comprehend."

THE CRESTED SCREECH

Some birds rarely speak,
While others like the *Crested Screech*
Rarely shut up,
Demanding to be heard.

Some squawk and talk the livelong day,
While others have nothing to say,
Shying away from speech.

What difference can this difference make?
Quite a lot when
Shutting up passively accepts
And speaking up assertively objects.

Whether to shut up and conceal
Or to speak up and reveal?
That is the question.

Whether to be known
Or to be unknown?
That is the question.

There are risks to keeping silent:
Condoning statements and stands
With which one doesn't actually agree.

There are risks to speaking out:
Others may take offense
And retaliate for blasphemy.

Besides,
Why chance speaking up
Against what everybody does
And what no one seems to mind?
What difference can it make?
What good can it do?
What's the point?

All it takes is one voice of dissent
To begin to right a historic wrong,
To begin to address a neglected need,
To begin to challenge an established view.

THE MALE GROUT

The *Grout*
Is not an aggressive bird
Except when two males
Get too close for comfort.

Then all kinds of posturing
For dominance occurs.

Beaks held high,
Heads thrown back
On coiled necks
Cocked to strike,
Two sudden adversaries
Try to intimidate each other,
Circling and vocalizing threats
Until the immanence of actual combat
Causes both to swim away
In a face saving retreat
(Each having stood up for
Whatever he was standing up for)
While the females
Continue to dive and feed
Apparently taking no heed
Of this display of masculinity
Because instinctively they know
It has nothing to do and everything to do with them.

Perhaps part of being female
Means letting males play at being men.

THE HOODED RAPTOR

Despite and because
Of all its formidable strengths,
The *Hooded Raptor* lacks courage
Since it knows no fear.

Fiercely defiant,
It is unable to be brave.

Not like most people.

Who's afraid of the Big Bad Wolf?
We all are.
Except the Wolf is different for each of us.

Who makes the Wolf more fearful?
We all do when we run away.

The Wolf says:
"If I catch you,
I will eat you up!"

But when we choose to run
We are already caught
And eaten up
By our own fear.

Making ourselves face what we fear
Is how we cause the Wolf to go away.

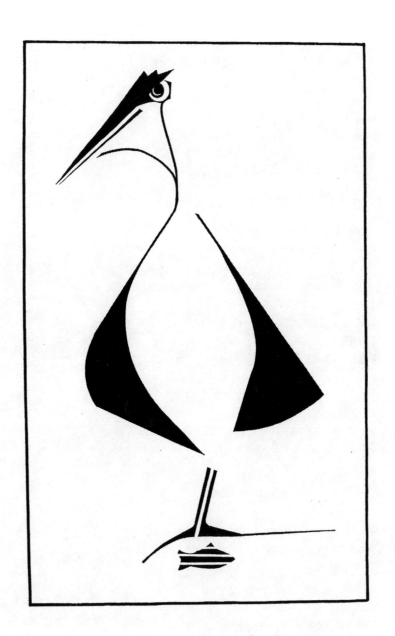

THE GRAY HERON

Seed-feeders forage for what to harvest.
Meat eaters roam for what to hunt.
Both stay on the move
Knowing nothing's gained by staying put.

Except the *Gray Heron*
Who's mastered the art of immobility.

Planting itself in the surroundings
As visible and invisible as a tree,
It is ignored by traveling creatures
Unable to conceive of a stationary threat.

Thus an errant fish,
Used to following its wandering ways,
Strays under the stalker's lethal gaze.

No surprise to the Gray Heron who knows
The world of motion weaves a web
Of ever-changing intersecting paths,
Soon or later one of which will lead to it.

Patience is rewarded with opportunity
Because most other creatures don't stay still.

Lack of timing or poor aim is the bird's mistake.
Success comes from waiting like a spider
And from striking like a snake.

THE TROPOLO

Once upon a time,
Not so very long ago,
It appeared the *Tropolo* was doomed.

When the humid region became parched and dry,
Lush forests withered from lack of rain,
Familiar fruit and seed dying as well,
Old feeding habits ceasing to sustain
As almost all the birds were lost
Except aberrant diversity
In a randomly selected few
Allowed adaptation to the new,
The immutable among them dying off
While mutant members found a niche and carried on.

What does it take for a species to survive?

Unless we change to fit
Evolving changes in our changing world,
The unchangeable among us shall become extinct.

THE TWIT

How does a bird decide at what altitude to fly?
Some aspire to rise no higher than the nearest tree,
While others climb the sky for thermal drafts on which to soar.

Soar?

The *Twit* has no use or need for that.
Probe the dirt is more like it.
Pry up cakes of decomposed debris
For beetles, grubs, and worms
Just waiting for discovery.

With food so plentiful at hand,
There is no need to leave the land.

Besides,
The law of earthly belonging
Ordains that what goes up must come down
Because even for birds there is no basis in the air.

No matter how lowly or lofty
One's ambition or attainment,
Sooner or later even the highest flyer
Is grounded when it comes home to roost.

THE PARROSET

A *Parroset* can act aggressively,
But does it feel angry?
A Parroset can act alarmed,
But does it feel afraid?
A Parroset can investigate possibilities,
But does it feel curious?
Two Parrosets can mate for life,
But do they feel love?

It's easy to impose
Our own sensibilities on birds
As we try to comprehend their alien ways,
Looking for similarities that connect us to each other.

Surely there's other kinship we can find.
After all, aren't we both living things?

Yes.

But for us,
Desire for kinship is selective.
While we cherish some forms of life,
We systematically exterminate others.
We prize "pretty" flowers but we poison "ugly" weeds.
We decide what survives based on our changing tastes and needs.

Better not to get on our bad side.

Arrogant is what we human beings are,
Presuming some of the natural world
Has value if it's valuable to us,
Discounting or destroying
What is not.

Surely everything has value or like us it wouldn't be.

Perhaps that's why,
When we get too close,
Parrosets act suspicious
(If suspicion is what they feel)
And immediately up and fly away.

Just because we've been their friend
Doesn't mean we're not their enemy today.

THE WILLOWICK

When the *Willowick*
Constructs a home,
It is to birth a family.

Once family is raised,
There is no further need for an abode.

When the last fledgling
Leaves the empty nest,
Parents simply fly away.

Nothing is left behind creating loss,
Nothing taken along to weigh them down,
Nothing of worth remains to tempt return.

When the past has served its purpose,
There is no further purpose to the past.
Next breeding season,
Another nest elsewhere will do.

Meanwhile,
Birds are secure without a place to call their own
Because they are secure within themselves,
Wherever in the world they happen to be.

It's how most people settle down
And most birds don't.

People need to have a home in which to nest,
But birds don't need a nest to have a home.

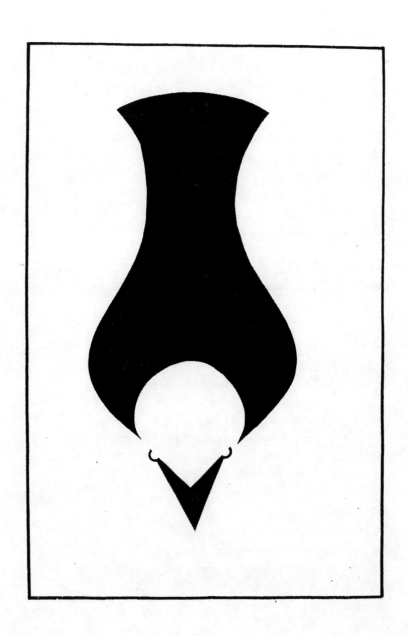

THE HOMILY

Can you imagine sitting on a nest like this,
On an insufferable mess like this,
Littered with debris
Collected from who knows where—
Bits of brightly colored plastic,
Pieces of shiny metal,
Shards of glass?

Why does the *Homily* accumulate such junk?
What purpose do such possessions serve?

To satisfy some need for ownership?
To express personal taste?
To measure wealth?
To please the eye?
To play?

And how does this agglomeration
Influence impressionable young?

Is it with them as it is with us,
Children coming to certain material conclusions
From coming to desire and depend on many things:
"What you have is who you are;"
"How much you have is what you're worth."
And the most important lesson
Taught by having all this stuff:
"A good consumer can never have enough."

THE EASTERN DRUMMER

The *Eastern Drummer*
Is a non-intrusive bird,
Not disturbing anyone,
Not disturbing anything,
Feeding quietly on what it finds,
Fitting in on its surrounding's terms,
Reaping whatever bounty the earth returns.

Not like us,
Too intelligent for our own good,
Too ambitious to let well enough alone,
To arrogant to submit to Mother Nature's rule,
We impose our will and force our living from the land.

The trouble is,
When we treat this place like we own this place
And subordinate it all to our hungry human needs;
When we treat this place like a resource to exploit
To support ourselves unmindful of the costs;
When we treat this place like it is deathless
And can tolerate no end of harm;
Then we have lost our place
In this small place in space,
The only place where we belong.

Better to follow
The rule of reciprocity:
If we want to be taken care of,
Then we have to take care of
What we want to take care of us.

So let's set the record straight:
The earth does *not* need people;
People need the earth.

THE AMERICAN ODDBIRD

Do all *American Oddbirds* truly look exactly alike?
That depends on who's doing the looking.

To another Oddbird,
The answer is definitely "No."
The endless variations are easy to see.
Only the ignorant are blind to diversity.

Enter the bird watcher.

More inclined to identify differences
Between species than within,
This species of human interest
Tends to make gross distinctions
Among birds of a similar feather—
Female, Male, Juvenile, Chick, and Egg.

Categorical thinking,
And categorical seeing,
And categorical hearing
Are tools to classify a bird,
Assigning it to a collective for recognition,
Thereby devaluing uniqueness it might possess.

When "one" becomes "one of them,"
Some "oneness" is lost.
When a flock of "them"
All appear the same
And cannot be told apart,
Social blindness can ensue.

Discrimination against a group begins
Where capacity to discriminate among individuals ends.

So, the test of a truly perceptive bird watcher is this:
"Having observed an individual Oddbird last week,
Would you know if you sighted it again?"

BONHAM'S GULL

Bonham's Gull does not come in out of the rain,
But scrunches down and ruffles up
And faces the wind's attack
Which drives the driving downpour
Down its sloping back,
The steadfast bird
Accepting stormy weather
With philosophical indifference,
Damp discomfort part of life to be endured.

Hunkering down
Is a serviceable skill
When conditions become worse,
Bearing its burdens of the moment
Until the moment's passed,
Or if it doesn't
Learning to accept
What's going to last.

In either case,
The Gull does not emotionally indulge
In frustration or disappointment,
Self-pity, worry, or rage,
Pessimism or despair,
To protest life's severity.

The way things are is the way things are meant to be.

THE GALLYMANDER

The *Gallymander* doesn't like to be disturbed
When it's doing something
Or when it's not.

Nor does it run from most intruders,
But stands them off with a pre-emptive glare
As if to say: "Bad mood, beware!"

Protective belligerence
Keeps trespassers away.

Like trying to find the right time
To raise concerns with a prickly adolescent:
A bad time,
Being given a hard time,
Is probably the best time
Parents are ever going to get.

THE SHORT-TAILED SKREET

The *Short-tailed Skreet*
Has no agenda when it flies
Except to seize opportunities when they arise,
Changing directions at a moment's notice
When the wind abruptly shifts
Or prey happens by,
Flying insects
Unable to predict
And so unable to avoid
A hunter so erratically effective.

Hard for control-seeking creatures like ourselves
To just let life provide as life unfolds.

We prefer imposing order
To make sure we secure
What we want
By making things happen,
Makers of our fate that we think we are.

Not like the Skreet,
Who trusts in serendipity
And exploits the gifts of chance.

Planning can be the enemy of possibility
Because no matter how far seeing,
It can also be shortsighted,
Overlooking
What is being given
For what we want to get.

THE TOPEK

Talk about ungrateful!
We provide
Food and shelter,
Keep predators at bay,
And is this the thanks we get?

Approaching a *Topek* in the farmyard,
It just turns away,
Beak in the air,
Without a backward glance,
Wanting nothing to do with us
After all the care we provide for it!

Acting so superior,
Treating us like we're only good
For serving and worth nothing more!

Is our only value in the seed we give?
How exploitive!
Treating us how we treat it!

But it's not lack of appreciation,
Only an unfair exchange:
"First you feed me,
Then I'll feed you."

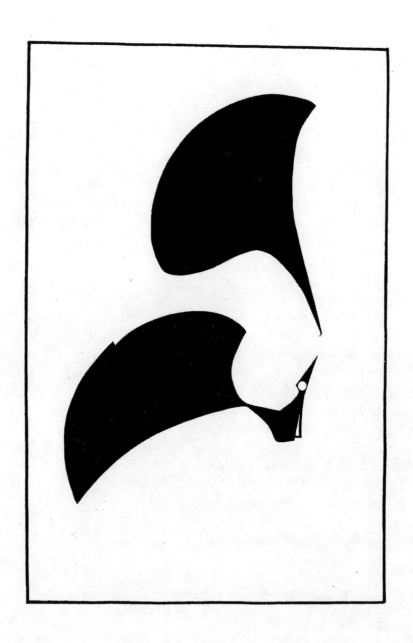

THE TARAHAWK

How can the *Tarahawk*
Be so kind and yet so cruel,
Nurturing its young one moment,
Then tormenting prey for play the next?

It is this mix of contrasts
That is so difficult to understand,
The mix that makes a contradiction of us all
Because each trait of character is really a continuum
From one pole to its polar opposite,
Each extreme defined
By absence of the other,
With a range of combinations in between.

We are both
Frail and strong,
Smart and stupid,
Confident and insecure,
Impulsive and restrained,
Serious and playful,
Careful and careless,
Lazy and industrious,
Truthful and dishonest,
Kind and cruel,
Even
Good and evil,
The hardest mix to accept
Because by accepting what we know is evil
We seem to be endorsing the enemy of human good.

But accepting is not the same as endorsing,
Permitting wrong for the sake of preserving right.
It simply admits our dependence on duality:
Without acknowledging the dark,
We cannot struggle for the light.

So we are constantly put to the test—
Tempted by our worst
While striving for our best,
The outcome an uneven compromise
Even for paragons of virtue we admire—
Those recovered sinners we revere as saints.

THE BITBIT

If there's no time but the present
And the immeasurable Now,
Then there's no time
To worry over future
Or to excavate the past.

If there's no reality
That's not concrete,
Then objectivity denies
Imagination and make-believe.

It's in this world of immediacy
Confined to physical sense,
That the *Bitbit* lives,
Unconcerned about
What really was,
What really is,
What will be,
What could be if,
What should occur,
What might have been,
All concerns of concern to us,
Who cannot expand our consciousness
Without shutting some of our awareness down.

THE STILTWELL

Consider this dichotomy:
Some birds are "Striders"
And some are "Jumpers."
Why?

Striders advance one foot before the other.
"Walking," we call it.

Jumpers advance both feet in unison.
"Hopping," we call it.

Couldn't whatever nature made up birds
Make up its mind?
Or is this difference
A lesson meant to teach?

Are Jumpers quicker to react
Because two legs working together
Create more speed of thrust than one?

Do Striders
Cover more distance across the ground,
Like the *Stiltwell* that runs as swiftly as it can fly?

Sprinting up the beach
Between the changing tides,
Stopping and starting to drill for food,
Racetracks vanishing in the liquid sand,
Puts the advantage of Striders on display.

No Jumper could hop as far as fast as that.

And as a Strider myself,
I tend to favor taking one step at a time,
That way if the front foot boldly errs,
The one behind can reconsider,
Bringing forward progress
To a prudent halt.

Not like Jumpers,
Fully committed to every leap they take,
Feeling confident they can jump out
Should they jump into a mistake.

THE PETTY SQUAWL

Why do *Petty Squawls* live in a flock
If all they want to do is bicker so?

Quarreling over food or perch or anything,
They get into one flap after another,
Waving their wings,
Fluffing up and huffing up,
Squawking threats or insults
Or whatever they have to say,
Creating a contagion of discontent,
Creating a rising babble of angry noise
That abruptly ceases when they take flight,
Only to recommence when they alight again.

If they dislike each other's company,
Why congregate?
For the sake of peace and quiet,
Why not separate?

Because peace and quiet cannot sustain a flock.
Because conflict is required for community.

Fighting brings them together
And sets them apart
Over differences
About which they agree to disagree.

Within creatures
And between creatures
There is no peaceable kingdom,
Only an unstable confederation
Of continuously warring states.

THE TAWNY SILLIS

What vanity!

Has the *Tawny Sillis*
Got nothing better to do
Than bathe and preen,
Bathe and preen,
Combing wet feathers
Into perfect place with its beak
Instead of just using it as a device to eat?

Whom is this grooming meant to impress?

Which is a human question I suppose,
Since when it comes to preening
And vanity and dress
Human beings really can't be beat.

Who else spends more time
Despairing or admiring their reflection?
Who else keeps altering image
To follow fashion's latest direction?
Who else attaches such importance to personal looks?

Why can't birds and people
Feel content to be unkempt?
In the great scheme of things,
Why should appearance matter?

Because everything matters.
Because nothing doesn't count.
Because everything is connected.
Because no part of us stands alone.

Because inside and outside,
Core and shell,
Each needs attention
For all to function well.

THE ATERAX

Some birds roost
Among a crush of their own kind,
At nightfall crammed onto a single tree
Taking crowded comfort in raucous density.

Others only socialize to mate,
Shunning all but each other's company.

Why this difference in sociability?

Why communal and solitary birds,
Public and private,
Joiners and loners,
The *Aterax*
One of the reclusive kind
Whose only sociability appears to be
Attacking those who trespass on its property.

To birds of this feather,
A good neighbor is one who keeps away.

It's complex,
This trade-off between social belonging
And relief from social contact,
But either way a bird chooses,
Isolation is to be expected.

The only real difference in sociability is this:
Choosing to live alone together or to live alone apart.

RALSTON'S JAY

Since *Ralston's Jay* is so adept
At extracting seeds
From shells,
One wonders:
Was it born already able,
Inheritance just waiting to perform?

No.

Innate capacity requires practice to be skilled.
Without effort, aptitude does only moderately well.

Talent is cheap that way,
Most people given more gifts
Than discipline and opportunity allow to grow.

Talent only achieves excellence through work,
The capacity for work the talent that counts most of all.

THE BI-COLORED RAVEN

How did the *Bi-colored Raven* get so wise?
From living so many years?

No.

Longevity can just as well lead to stupidity.
Something about how the Raven thinks
Sets it apart from other birds.

To demonstrate,
I toss a sparkling gem
Tumbling across the ground,
Then discretely step away,
Stand still and wait.

My distance assured,
The Raven drops down
To contemplate what it has found.

Other birds
Ignore any object
Obviously unfit to eat,
But not the hungry Raven
Who has an appetite for the unknown.

Although not food to nourish the body,
Such unusual brightness is food for thought.

So with the deportment of a connoisseur,
The Raven slowly circles around the thing,
Giving it due consideration from many angles,
At last poking with its beak for touch and smell,
Picking it up to test the weight and balance,
Letting it go to judge the speed of fall,
Cocking its head to review the data,
Slowly digesting what is learned.

Bird as scientist,
Is that how wisdom grows?
Curiosity determined to discover,
What natural mystery will not disclose.

THE GANDER

The *Gander*'s role
Is to patrol its territory
And to protect its mate
Who incubates the eggs,
Gently shifting to warm them all,
Parental responsibilities divided thus
According to some secret sexual directive
That makes gender differences very clear,
Except when she fiercely defends her brood,
Or he relieves her nurturing presence on the nest.

Elusive,
This business of sex role distinction:
Just when a difference is considered fixed,
Designations become unexpectedly switched.

Why isn't sexuality as simple as it seems—
One way or the other,
This way or that,
Either/or?

Because in every individual sexuality is mixed,
Male and female potentials embedded in them each
Creating an infinite variety of sexual definitions—
As many ways of being female
As there are women,
As many ways of being male
As there are men,
As many was of being masculine
As there are women,
As many ways of being feminine
As there are men.

THE SCIMITAR

What caused the *Scimitar*
To be so acrobatic—
Able to hover,
Fly backwards,
Perch upside down,
And somersault through the air?

Without this special agility
It could not cope with conditions
Which prohibit ordinary flight—
Through an impenetrable world
Of interlacing vines and creepers
Where laden branches from above
Wed lush profusion from below
Creating a hopeless tangle
As dense as jungle,
As confusing as a maze,
Pitch black blind at night,
Twilight dim during the day.

Here are no byways
Or established flight paths to follow,
Only momentary openings through which to dart
And unexpected obstacles to instantaneously evade.

The Scimitar adjusts to its surroundings,
As do we all.

We aren't self-made
So much as we are shaped by circumstance.

THE HARVESTER

The clean-up crew is here,
A gang of *Harvesters*
Removing road-kill from the road.

"Scavengers" we scorn them,
Carnivores who never actually slay,
Feeding on refuse hunters leave behind,
On victims of accidents,
On losers to disease.

Easy to view such feasting with disgust
(How can they pick at rotting flesh?)
And yet we eat what's in decay,
And flesh is still flesh,
Whether of animals,
Of vegetables,
Of seeds,
Of fruit.

Harvesters all is what we are,
Serving the larger needs of existence
In which matter must keep changing form,
And life and death both have important roles to play
Because composing and decomposing,
Consuming and being consumed,
Is how nature maintains itself.

Everything that dies becomes food for life.
Without the dead the living can't survive.

THE KUA KUA

Not every bird takes flight
By taking to the air.

The *Kua Kua* for example
Chases down lizards and snakes for prey,
Escaping enemies of its own by running away.

A terrestrial bird except in emergencies,
The Kua Kua prefers what's solid underfoot,
Far more substantial than the unsubstantial air,
Aware that solids are the vast exception in the universe,
The earth a tiny speck of matter hung in space,
We passengers along for part of the ride,
So long as the ride lasts,
Until some random asteroid
Crashes through our atmosphere
And explodes into our crust,
Snuffing us dinosaurs out
With a suffocating cloud of dust,
Or we eventually orbit too close to the sun
And a final blaze of glory or inglory does us in.

Who wants to live with such scenarios in mind?

Not I.

Grounded like the Kua Kua
Is how I prefer to be and more,
Believing that choice and conduct,
And how we treat and help each other,
All have significance in the here and now,
Believing that life in its variety is worth preserving
And a better future worth preparing and striving for.

THE CROKER

What's it like to be an urban bird like the *Croker*,
Living among people who inhabit land by paving it over,
Resurfacing the earth with what the human mind invents,
Towering structures of steel and stone and glass,
Streets and highways of asphalt and concrete,
Allowing little room for token greenery
So nary a bird can afford a tree—
Cities an arid place to live?

As we have done to ourselves,
We have done to our fellow creatures
Who have been urbanized and ostracized,
Adapting to the noise and density and smog
Or have fled for more open space
Crowding up at a slower pace.

No escaping human evolution
For other creatures or ourselves,
Victims of our own ingenuity,
Growing forward
Because there is no going back,
Creating new terms on which to live,
Less connected with our natural surroundings,
But more technologically advanced and equipped.

Human progress is a mix of possibility and penalty
Even for the Croker who is now better off
And worse off than before,
Finding ample roosting space
And shelter on the edges and ledges of things,
Diet dependent on refuse human beings throw away.

THE MOUNTAIN WREN

For the *Mountain Wren*,
Building a nest is incremental work:
Scouting about for a likely site,
Then gathering diverse materials
For each phase of manufacture—
Twigs for structure,
Grass for insulation,
Softer stuff on which to lay the eggs.

Philosophically,
Questions concerning nest conception are complex.

Consider:
How does one fix a true starting point for its creation?
Does the process start as soon as the first twig is laid,
Or does the process start when the first twig is made?

Perhaps beginnings begin before beginning has begun
(And endings only end after ending is done.)

And if there's no clear beginning or clear end,
Then how did anything come to be?

The answer is simply this:
If nothing can come from nothing,
Then something was always there;
And if something was always there,
Then there was nothing to begin with.

THE HAPPY FALLOW

Is the *Happy Fallow*
As happy as it looks,
Or is that permanent grin
Only as fixed and sincere as a politician's smile?

No more true or to be trusted than that.

Or is it no smile at all,
But simply an artifact of the beak's design
On which we project warm feelings we wish were there?

Declaring superiority over "lower" species,
We get lonely to connect with other creatures,
Domesticating those who live with us and give to us
In exchange for comforts of dependency that we provide.

Dog lovers tend to believe they are loved by dogs,
But is that wagging attachment really love?
Cat lovers demand less affection,
Recognizing rubbing against them
And sitting upon them and purring
As proprietary acts of marking and claiming,
Announcing to any rival cats just who owns whom.

Bird lovers just look for the love of it,
Expecting no bird love in return.
And yet,
It's hard for even a hard-hearted bird lover
Not to smile back at the Happy Fallow,
All the while knowing it's absurd
To conceive of a smiling bird.

THE DRILL WEAVER

Watching a *Drill Weaver*
Startle and flee at my approach,
Putting up a flurry of other wings,
I appreciate how quickly many can alert to one.

There is safety in flocks
Because each member acts sentinel for the rest.

Spying a devil cat on the prowl,
A single bird takes to the air
Exploding the rest
Into instant flight
Without knowing why,
Without having to know why,
To fly away when feeding was so good,
Trusting in the fright of one to protect them all.

Fear can be so wise.

Rising in unison
They escape they know not what
And if there was no danger,
There was no harm,
And if danger there was,
No harm was done.

Then from the safety of their roosts
The watch begins,
The communal safety watch,
All awaiting signs that all is clear.

At last one daring bird
Dares to revisit the abandoned ground,
Then several cautious others flutter down,
Then the rest freely reassemble as before,
Since the passing threat I posed
Has safely passed.

It's a principle of interdependence:
Each bird must trust
The instincts of each other
If everyone is going to survive.

THE CHICKOREE

Furtive and quick and shy,
The unassuming *Chickoree*
Yields to more aggressive birds,
Stealing leftovers they leave behind,
Darting in and out at a moment's notice,
Seizing the fleeting opportunity to stay alive.

To be so low on the pecking order
Is to be at a disadvantage,
Or is it?

Because the Chickoree appears to thrive.

Ignored by more imposing birds,
It is protected by obscurity.
Not worth attention,
It is left alone.

To do what?

To exercise ingenuity,
Discovering unlikely sources
Of nourishment in unlikely places,
Food more dominant birds either fail to see
Or deem too scant for foraging.

Ever alert
To overlooked possibilities,
The Chickoree makes out very well.

In nature and in human nature,
Those who can't compete for the ordinary
Often learn to exploit the unusual to survive.

THE BROAD-BILLED BOOBY

If they were cruelly human,
Other birds would laugh
At the *Broad-billed Booby*,
Would ridicule its rolling gait
Lumbering down the beach
Staggering off balance
From one flat foot to another
Almost tipping over from side to side,
Wings flailing for purchase on the air
In a desperate run for flight,
Failing as often as not,
Tumbling to a clumsy conclusion,
Falling down instead of rising aloft,
Undiscouraged righting itself to try again.

Why design a bird for such embarrassment?
Is this some kind of bad joke?
I mean, where's the good?

The good is this.

Come the monsoons,
When every living winged thing
Is blasted from the glowering sky,
When even hardy sea birds feel daunted
And seek shelter from the everlasting gale,
Behold the Broad-billed Booby

Flying into the fiercest wind
And holding its own
Steady as it goes,
Wearing the wind's resistance down,
Stubbornly undeterred from its self-appointed course
To its chosen destination,
Storm be damned.

Who laughs at the Broad-billed Booby now?

Perhaps all Nature's disabilities are double-edged
And there's no cursed awkwardness
That under favorable circumstance
Does not become a blessed gift.

WENDELL'S STORK

With slow sweeping strokes
Wendell's Stork swims through the evening air,
Skimming across dark water to its familiar roost,
Vast wings extended for a final glide back home,
Touching down so lightly
The branch barely sags
As the bird ruffles up
And settles down
For the night.

Wondering at the beauty
Of this effortless flight,
One wonders:
"Whoever Wendell was,
Did Wendell wonder too?"

As for the bird,
As its reward for being found,
In the name of scientific discovery
It was consecrated with the finder's name.

What human vanity!

How can we claim discovery of something new
When what we found was already there?

THE COLEOPSIS

Why do we admire birds like the *Coleopsis?*
Does the exotic and elaborate plumage
Especially compel our view?

Would we be less responsive
If the bird were plainly dressed and colored drab?

If so,
What manner of prejudice is discriminating taste?
And who decides what visually inspires?

Is beauty in the object beheld
Or in the eye of the beholder?

Is it universally apparent
Or just personally appealing?

Is it abiding
Or is it fickle like fashion?

Our appreciation of birds,
Like our appreciation of so much in life,
Is testimony to the superficial way we look.

We view the world
From the outside in,
Not from the inside out.

THE WATER WETZELL

Most birds fish when they're hungry,
But the *Water Wetzell* also seems to fish for sport.

Having caught and eaten its fill,
It keeps going back for more,
Leaving flapping bodies
Gasping on the shore
For awaiting scavengers,
Because in nature nothing goes to waste.

Killing for play?

Some humans love to do it—
Trapping, shooting, angling for game—
Their simple objective murderously clear
Except this fatal goal is not entirely the point
Because when the cruel trap isn't sprung,
When the gun sights no excuse to fire,
When fish refuse to bite or strike,
The experience still fulfills.

Hard for the enemies of deadly gaming
To appreciate the value of a failed quest.
But the trapper, hunter, or fisherman
Never comes home empty handed,
Only full,
Only laden
With more to tell
About what did or didn't happen
In this latest episode of challenge, choice, and chance.

Long after the adventure's over,
The glory of the story
Lingers on.

Another chapter of outdoor romance.

THE SQUAT-TAILED OWL

Escaping the sun,
The *Squat-tailed Owl*
Seems an unlikely predator.

Short and stout and sluggish,
Still as the perch it slumps upon,
To all appearances unthreatening
Unless you know what to be frightened of,
As smaller animals and birds have learned to be.

They know the difference between the little owl
Is as simple as the difference between night and day,
Between a hunter as swift and silent and lethal in the dark
As it is safe to ignore or even torment when it is blind to light.

And they know to watch out for the dawn,
Keeping their guard up at the changing of the guard,
Because an owl that has come up empty-taloned
And rests with its eyes squinted shut,
May still hunger for a meal
Before repose.

No to see well is not the same as not to see at all.
Less of a danger is still danger none-the-less.

So creature wisdom has concluded this:
In early morning,
Beware a dozing owl.

Half asleep is also half awake.

THE COMMON GREBE

Between hazards of nature
And the hunger of predators,
It's rare for a pair of *Common Grebes*
To nurture an entire brood into young adults.

Given accidents,
Nest robbers and hidden things
Pulling the innocent under so they drown,
Perhaps only one chick survives to maturity,
Sole focus of both parents' parental care
Because parenting means being there,
Putting in time and effort and work
To nourish, educate, and protect
Until sufficient growth
Can fend for itself.

Then late one Spring day,
The young leaves never to return,
Never looking, coming, or giving back,
Within a year not even recognizing parents if they met,
Treating them as strangers, territorial invaders, rivals for food.

Each generation is responsible for bearing and preparing the
next.
Neither generation is concerned for each other
Once they stop sharing a nest.

There's a different model for extended family living
Human parents often want their children told:
"First the old care-take their young,
Then the young care-take their old."

THE ROSE CHERRYMOUNT

What's this apparent courtesy
When a *Rose Cherrymount*
Meets another?

Dropping one wing,
Each starts this bowing thing,
This social bobbing up and down
Before both parties at last feel free
To go their separate ways.

What greeting ritual is this?
What are they trying to find out?
What is the value of this exchange?

Something about how they relate:
"If we're not okay together,
Then we're not okay apart."

"I am well if we are well,"
They seem to say.

How unlike us.

Instead of always asking: "How are you?"
Rose Cherrymounts keep asking: "How are we?"

THE COLLARED EAGLE

Sooner or later
We must all face the *Collared Eagle*,
In whatever form it takes,
For a full accounting
Of what little we have learned
During what little time we've had,
Summing up our human good and human bad:

"Between us,
There's no higher power than the power of love;"

"Within us,
There's no limit to the inquiring and inventive mind;"

"Beyond us,
There's no ruling goal or guiding truth on which we all agree;"

"Among us,
There's no savior from the savagery of our own kind;"

"Individually we do much right,
But collectively commit more wrong."

THE TOLLY BARBER

Why do birds fight?

To control space,
To compete for food,
To assert dominance,
To defend their young,
To win a winning mate.

Even a bird as docile as the *Tolly Barber*
Can become aggressive
When self-interest
Or survival are at stake.

Conflict is natural,
Conflict is not wrong,
Conflict is not going away,
Conflict is how creatures get along.

When differences
Cause opposing parties to disagree,
Conflict is how they manage this diversity.

Will warring human conflict ever end?

Yes.

Lasting peace will at last be won
When the war to end all wars
Destroys the earth
For everyone.

THE TINTERMITE

With the temper of a shrew
And the tiny size to match,
The *Tintermite* attacks
All intruders of its space,
Flying into the face
Of a feral cat
(Caught by surprise)
Pecking its nose and eyes,
Escaping its fangs and claws
Until the puzzled beast withdraws,
Choosing a less annoying way around.

How can a bantam bird evict a wild cat?

With fierce intent
That lets no trespass go,
That brooks no opposition,
That assails foes with abandon,
That totally commits to gain control,
That never yields so long as it has breath,
That fights without concern for hurt or fear of death.

Small might prevails
Because aggression
Is not greater strength,
But a ferocious attitude:
"At any cost, my will be done!"

THE TALISMAN

With long tail and legs,
Large wattle, wings, and beak,
The *Talisman* is hard to miss
But even harder to catch.

Faster than most four-footed enemies,
When a foolish predator does run it down
There's hell to pay fighting this formidable bird
Now fighting for its life
With kicks to fell a tree,
With beating wings to crush,
With a beak to eviscerate like a knife.

Why would any creature hunt a Talisman?
How could the challenge justify the cost?
Why dare the certain danger?

Because trophy ambition is a gamble,
Like all gambling after more,
Venturing great risk
For great reward's allure.

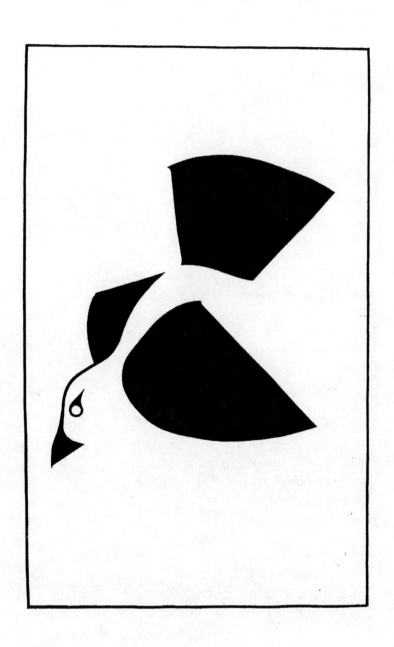

THE KILKEN

What can the *Kilken* teach us as it dives?

That it takes less effort to fall
Than it does to rise?

It can be harder to *create* than to destroy.
It can be harder to *contest* than go along.
It can be harder to be *brave* than run away.
It can be harder to *confront* than to avoid.
It can be harder to *speak out* than to shut up.
It can be harder to *confess* than to deny.
It can be harder to *listen* than ignore.
It can be harder to *persist* than to give up.
It can be harder to *remember* than forget.
It can be harder to be *moderate* than extreme.
It can be harder to be *faithful* than betray.
It can be harder to be *honest* than deceive.
It can be harder to *trust* than to suspect.
It can be harder to *accept* than to prejudge.
It can be harder to be *fair* than to cheat.
It can be harder to *work* than to play.
It can be harder to *forgive* than to resent.
It can be harder to be *thankful* than ungrateful.
It can be harder to do *right* than what feels good.

So this is what one learns:
The easy way may be quicker and easier,
But the harder way yields more lasting returns.

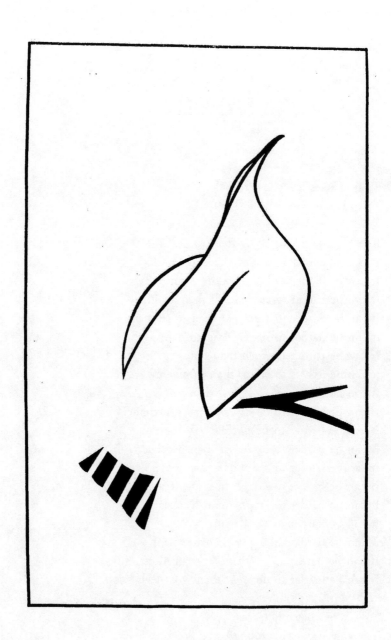

THE MORNING DOVE

Each dawn I hear the velvet tones of the *Morning Dove*
Warbling smoothly, insistently, and low,
A chorus of velvet voices
Softly lulling me awake
As morning fills with light
And the unrelenting challenge
Of making a living begins once more.

Sometimes,
My weary inclinations
Are reluctant to relinquish sleep,
Even resent another cycle of survival
Come round with its demands again,
Until I'm gently reminded
Of what I have received.

So many Morning Doves
Can't all be wrong:
Surely the gift of a new day
Deserves the celebration of a song.

THE JACKALAN

All parents are given the same dire warning:
"Unattended chicks may fall victim to the *Jackalan.*"

What predator is this
That feeds on young of other birds,
Exploiting lapses in family vigilance,
Waiting for unwise and unwary,
Impulsive and adventurous youth
To straggle behind or wander ahead
Of parental oversight and safekeeping?

Danger is like that,
Always hovering around us,
Like the Jackalan infinitely patient,
Biding its time for tragic opportunity to strike.

Do everything we can,
Parental protection is insufficient,
And even if it were complete it wouldn't be enough
Because protection is no preparation
For independent living
When grown children leave
To face life's perils on their own.

THE BANDIT

The *Bandit*
Gets away with stealing
Except when victims unite
To drive the hungry thief away.

Preying on less aggressive birds,
Chasing them off their catch or kill,
The Bandit lets them find what it will eat.

"What's yours is mine
Unless you want to fight,"
Is how the bird behaves,
And it's partly wrong
And partly right.

After all,
Why should anything belong to anyone?
Why doesn't everything belong to all of us?

And if it does,
Then stealing's no more wrong than ownership
(Private possession the theft of public good)
Because both are a form of robbery.

So much for personal property,
Which is not what one is entitled to,
But what has the will and power to defend.

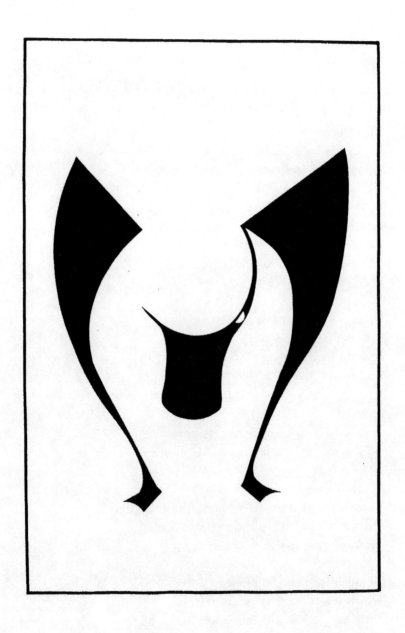

THE TATTERSOL

The *Tattersol* doesn't blink at life
But stares at whatever happens
Because how life unfolds
Is simply how life is.

Wishes to the contrary
Cannot turn the bird's honest gaze aside.

Whatever it sees has nowhere to hide.

How different from people
Whose vision is limited
To what they can emotionally bear
And to what they will intellectually accept.

If truth is a source of pain or fear,
Or runs counter to cherished beliefs,
It becomes inadmissible to the intolerant mind
And the hurt or frightened person
In self-defense will deny:
"It's not happening;"
"It didn't happen;"
"It won't happen;"
"It's not true,"
(No matter what
Reason or reality have to say.)

Denial is how we limit what we know
To what we want or do not want to know,
Because nothing is as blinding as the truth:
Sometimes when we see it,
See it we will not.

THE HOBHILL CRANE

First,
We drive a bird to the edge of extinction
By destroying its habitat
As we create our own,
And then at the last minute
We decide we want the species back,
And so begins a fight to reclaim what's been lost
At great social effort, political upheaval, and financial expense.

So we are down (at last count)
To ten nesting pairs of *Hobhill Cranes*
Who have no idea how precarious their numbers have become,
Except they do get tired of seeing the same old faces
In the same old migratory places:
"Don't you wish Julia and Fred
Would go breed somewhere else instead?"

Then to make matters worse,
There are all these unbirdlike intruders
Hovering about and sneaking around and spying,
Even prying into nests (which are none of their business)
And generally annoying and disturbing and distressing
Creatures who propagate best when left alone.

Why don't these interlopers go elsewhere?

Because we don't think of ourselves as intruders.
This earth is ours and we don't mean to go away
Since it's our only hold in boundless space.

But just suppose we gradually did decline
And were down to the last ten nesting pairs of people,
Would any other species step up to save a dying human race?

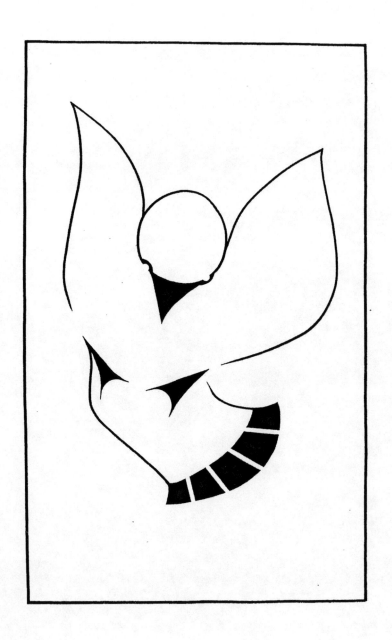

THE SPANNER

The *Spanner* cautiously descends
Gradually flapping slower,
Feet tentatively reaching out to land,
Grasping a bending branch bending lower,
Testing the untested perch for reliable support,
Wings at last pulling in as full weight finally bears down,
A bird that won't commit to what it cannot absolutely trust.

Wary believers is what wild birds are.
Scary believers is what people are.

Whatever truth is,
Once people are convinced they possess it,
They become possessed by the certainty of their belief.

What was open to question
Can become closed to discussion,
Argument considered ignorant or wrong.

The problem with true beliefs
Are the true believers that they spawn.

And we are all true believers in something.

At least that's my true belief.

THE KOOKEROO

Why don't smaller birds leave the *Kookeroo* alone?
Since it doesn't bother anyone,
Why bother it?

But they can't resist
Mocking it with noise,
Driving it from its roost,
Flying after it as it flies off,
Ganging up on a solitary bird
That backs off rather than fighting back,
Relying on strength of numbers in their attack,
Not to injure just to pester and harass,
Not meaning to be mean so much
As meaning to have fun.

Fun for whom?

Teasing is more pleasing
To the teasers than the teased.

THE BULBULPIT

When we give a living thing a name,
Do we add meaning or do we take meaning away?

Do we enhance our appreciation of it,
Or do we diminish our wonder in response?

Do we broaden our perspective,
Or do we close it down?

And whatever the tradeoff,
Is language worth the price we pay—
To codify perception for communication's sake?

So seeing this exotic bird
We simply say: "There's a *Bulbulpit*."
Now we can tell other people what we saw,
Creating a common reference with the common name we gave.

Naming of birds is particularly confusing—
More so than with mammals, insects, reptiles, or fish
Because the titles we confer are often less naturally descriptive.

Call a bird
By my favorite bird name, Bobolink,
And what have we done?
Resorted to a combination of nonsense and poetry
To make a bird seem humorous
Or even sound absurd.

Perhaps we just enjoy giving a fanciful name
For the playful pleasure naming gives us in return?

THE DARK-SHOULDERED PIGEON

When the *Dark-shouldered Pigeon*
Isn't feeding,
And isn't mating,
And isn't sleeping,
It is usually roosting—
Settling down on some elevated perch,
On a ledge or limb or wire,
In a state of complacency.

Why?

Why would any creature
Want to waste time roosting
When there's so much doing to be done?

Exactly.
Roosting is unproductive,
And that's the point.

No needs to fulfill,
No plans to pursue,
No obligations to honor,
No ambitions to achieve,
No chores to complete,
No schedules to meet,

No work to perform,
No diversions to play,
Just time to observe
The sights of the world,
And the sounds of the world,
And one's sense of the world passing by.

"Boring!"
Complain the young:
"There's nothing to do!"

But aging changes youth.
We begin by seeking excitement,
But we end by searching for peace.

As I grow older,
I grow more content to roost.

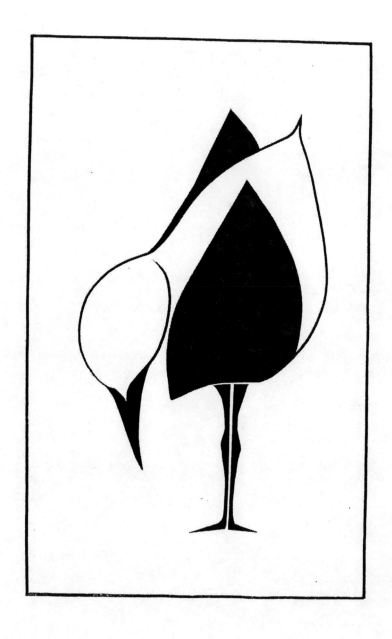

THE ORDALEE

Why is the *Ordalee* so painfully particular,
Meticulously clearing ground
Before laying its nest,
Picking and pecking the surface pebble-clean,
Stamping and tamping the remaining granules smooth?

Is a home that's not immaculately kept
Not worth the keeping?
Without domestic order
Is there no sense of self-control?

Between two partners,
One who loves disarray
And one who prizes order,
Marriage can be a protracted fight
About whether neatness or messiness is right.

The question is:
On whose terms are they going to live?
On those one is given or on those one gives?

Perhaps that's why the Ordalee
Mates based on similarity,
With one of its own kind.

Not about to change its habits,
It can't afford a partner who will disagree:
"For a harmonious marriage,
You must believe and behave like me."

THE WINDSHRIFT

Along Saint Gordon's Strait,
A raging sea assaults the coast relentlessly.

In this incessantly embattled place,
The *Windshrift* turns adversity
To its advantage by turning
Hardship for others
Into opportunity,
Intercepting wind-driven birds,
Battered by turbulence,
Barely aloft,
Desperate for land.

Flying out to welcome them,
It plucks the exhausted from the sky,
Transporting them surely if not safely down
To the shore they hoped to reach,
To an isolated shelter
On a lonely beach.

Some predators thrive
On appearing to rescue
Those struggling to survive.

THE MUCKANDER

The *Muckander* grovels in the ground
Because digging must be done
If food is to be found.

Shoveling up dirt,
It mines the laden earth
For larvae, bugs, and worms.

Bring life down to the basics
And making a living
Means earning enough to eat.

To that end,
Most of us grub for what we need,
Spending long hours in work,
Paid, unpaid, or both,
As conditions vary,
Sometimes easy,
Sometimes full of stress,
Some days taking everything
We have to give just to survive,
Knowing survival's no big deal,
Taken for granted since it's required.

Taken for granted?

Think about it.

When was the last time you had someone say:
"Congratulations, you just made it through another day!"

THE UPSTART

Flitting
In and out,
Up and down,
Here and there,
Back and forth,
Around and about,
Pausing but never stopping,
Ever eager to be on the move again:
Perhaps the *Upstart*
Can't stand being bored,
Or the aloneness stillness brings,
Or fears missing out on this by doing that,
Or finds what's next more alluring than what came last.

What does such restlessness have to teach?

To get the most out of life:
Go everywhere now,
Stay nowhere very long,
Keep changing your mind,
And be as quick about it as you can.

THE VECTOR

Taken, tamed, and trained
To hunt upon command,
To kill and leave its kill,
Rewarded for returning
To its master's hand
With a morsel to eat,
An approving word,
And a soothing touch,
The *Vector* is taught obedience,
But not too much.

How does the handler have such control?

The handler doesn't.

The lion tamer
Putting big cats through tricks,
The falconer
Fowling with hawks,
The parent
Of an impulsive child,
All come to understand
They can't control what's wild.

There's no control,
One creature over another,
Only cooperation between the two:
The handler giving commands,
The handled granting consent,
Together creating the illusion
Of one making another do.

THE ROYAL MANDARIN

Modesty aside,
How could any female resist
The male *Royal Mandarin* in full display
Of brilliant plumage and elaborate dress,
Naturally designed to sexually impress?

And yet,
In sexual conquest
It's hard to determine
Just who has conquered whom?

The male parading in his finery,
Or the female who is relatively plain?

The male who expresses interest,
Of the female with better things to do?

Winning ways
Can be both passive and aggressive,
'Hard to get' as alluring as 'hot pursuit.'

And no one is more easily seduced than the great seducer,
Seduced into believing he or she is irresistibly attractive to the
    other sex.

THE SPREAD EAGLE

To protect the *Spread Eagle*
We must preserve its habitat;
But to preserve its habitat
We must limit our own,
Leaving enormous tracts of land untouched,
Undeveloped despite our hungry human needs.

Largest of its kind,
This bird's great size
Confers a benefit and exacts a cost:
Easily dominating smaller creatures,
It needs far more range and food to live.

Advantage gained by greater strength
Is lost by all it takes to keep it strong.

Many square miles of land to hunt
Are necessary to support a single bird
Which cannot afford to live on less,
While we keep wanting more.

So competing priorities come into play.

As our population continues to grow,
Adaptation favors consuming less
And living in less space,
Because as human life evolves,
Acquiring much may be the way to go,
But requiring little becomes the way to stay.

THE ROCK LIMPET

Seasoned sailors take warning:
"When *Rock Limpets* roost together,
Two days out is heavy weather."

This prediction
Is dismissed as superstition
By more reasonable skeptics:
"How could a bird forecast a storm?"

Then when sullen clouds begin to gather and hang low,
When the sun is blotted out and daylight dims to gray,
When the breeze stiffens and the temperature drops,
When ranks of rising waves march toward the shore,
When lightening strikes and stirs the sea to foam,
When thunder claps its ominous applause,
When visibility is lost to driving rain,
Then sailors simply shrug:
"Rock Limpets never lie."

So the question is:
How do we tell anything for sure?

Whether we rely
On logic or intuition,
On objective evidence
Or theoretical imagination,
On scientific method or religious explanation,
On time honored superstition or mystical sense
To determine what is real and right and true,
All certainty of any kind depends on faith,
Trusting whatever means we choose
For being adequately shown
What is actually known.

THE COCKRELL

The *Cockrell* carries its young upon its back
Until free adventure becomes more alluring
Than a free ride,
The riders deciding to try
Independent transportation instead.

Dependence is a lot to give up
Both for parents and for child.

Parents relinquish control,
But are released from responsibility.
The child relinquishes support,
But gains freedom for self-determination.

After holding on has given way to letting go,
Both parties to the old dependence
May still have moments of regret.

Parents can mourn the loss of influence
Over conduct with which they now disagree.
The child can miss the services of days gone by
As relentless demands must relentlessly be met.

One reason life is so confoundingly complex
Is that our choices are a constant compromise,
One trade-off after another
As we make better changes
And creative solutions

Which only become substitutions,
One set of problems and payoffs for another,
    ing up some value to get what we want more,
At best the new conditions preferable to the old,
Offsetting worth of what's been given up.

Thus the price of progress is always pain
(Why social reform wounds as it heals)
Because some loss is paid for every gain.

.

THE UPLAND SHROUD

Most wild birds
Are wise enough not to relax,
Because eternal vigilance
Prevents surprise attacks.

As for sleep,
They tend to sleep on the alert,
Thus 'not awake' does not mean 'not aware.'

"I was only half-asleep," we joke
When dozing off in someone's company.

But sleeping half-asleep
Is no laughing matter to a wild bird
Like the *Upland Shroud*
Which goes to sleep
With one eye open
While the other's shut,
Treating sleep as a compromise
Between getting rested
And staying alive.

THE SPECTRAL

Shunning the sunlight,
Shunning the starlight,
Shunning the moonlight,
The *Spectral* glides across still water
Cloaked in shadows of the murky shore,
Dark plumage camouflaging with the night,
Invisible to all but its own kind.

"No, it doesn't!"
"Yes, it does!"

You see,
Bird watchers disagree
Whether this phantom bird could actually be.

Unbelievers among them call it pure fantasy:
"If a bird can't be observed then it can't exist.
Wishful thinkers is what you are!"

But Believers insist on the power of possibility:
"If a bird can be imagined it might come true.
Cynical skeptics is what you are!"

Who is right?
Perhaps both.

Just as history is partly fiction,
And fiction is partly history,
So it takes both fact and fancy
To create what we consider real.

THE DEAD BIRD

Beholding a *dead bird* always comes as a surprise.
Why?

The world is full of birds
But we rarely see them born
(Because nest security relies on secrecy.)
And we rarely see them die
(Because they do so privately,
Or do we just deny?)

Of course,
We are more drawn to watching birth than death.
Births are so promising,
While endings are so—
So what?
So sad?
So frightening?
So mysterious?
So perplexing not to know
The one answer we yearn to know:
What happens to us after life expires?

Seeing a dead bird is arresting.
It stops our eye from wandering
And fixes it upon our own mortality.

Life as we know it is not forever.
We are cut down by accident or intent.
We are fatally stricken by disease.
Or we simply age into decay
Like falling leaves when our fall is done,
Like this limp reminder of a living bird
Which has become liberated at last
Because the other side of loss,
Even the loss of life,
Is freedom—
Freedom from
And freedom for.
At the end we shall begin.
We have died before and we shall die again.

FINIS
(Next: *FISH OF DREAMS)*

BVG